The Young Rosciad [i.e. W. H. W. Betty], an admonitory poem well-seasoned with Attic salt ... By Peter Panglos, etc.

Peter Panglos, William Betty

The BiblioLife Network

This project was made possible in part by the BiblioLife Network (BLN), a project aimed at addressing some of the huge challenges facing book preservationists around the world. The BLN includes libraries, library networks, archives, subject matter experts, online communities and library service providers. We believe every book ever published should be available as a high-quality print reproduction; printed on- demand anywhere in the world. This insures the ongoing accessibility of the content and helps generate sustainable revenue for the libraries and organizations that work to preserve these important materials.

The following book is in the "public domain" and represents an authentic reproduction of the text as printed by the original publisher. While we have attempted to accurately maintain the integrity of the original work, there are sometimes problems with the original book or micro-film from which the books were digitized. This can result in minor errors in reproduction. Possible imperfections include missing and blurred pages, poor pictures, markings and other reproduction issues beyond our control. Because this work is culturally important, we have made it available as part of our commitment to protecting, preserving, and promoting the world's literature.

GUIDE TO FOLD-OUTS, MAPS and OVERSIZED IMAGES

In an online database, page images do not need to conform to the size restrictions found in a printed book. When converting these images back into a printed bound book, the page sizes are standardized in ways that maintain the detail of the original. For large images, such as fold-out maps, the original page image is split into two or more pages.

Guidelines used to determine the split of oversize pages:

• Some images are split vertically; large images require vertical and horizontal splits.
• For horizontal splits, the content is split left to right.
• For vertical splits, the content is split from top to bottom.
• For both vertical and horizontal splits, the image is processed from top left to bottom right.

1641 g. 29.

THE

YOUNG ROSCIAD,

AN ADMONITORY

POEM,

WELL-SEASONED WITH ATTIC SALT,

CUM NOTIS VARIORUM.

BY

PETER PANGLOSS, Esq. L.L.D. & A.S.S.

Clytus.———" Oh monstrous Vanity!"

Alexander.———" You flatter me."

Clytus.———" They do indeed!"

Nat. Lee.

LONDON:

Published by W. GORDON, No. 357, Oxford-Street,

And may be had of all other Booksellers.

1805.

Printed by J. Roach, }
Russel-Court. }

EPISTLE DEDICATORY.

To the Proprietors of the Theatres Royal,

Drury-Lane and Covent-Garden.

Gentlemen,

FROM the intimacy that has ſubſiſted between us for ſome years, I confeſs, with equal candour and pride, that I owe almoſt my exiſtence and preſervation to your foſtering hands. Though I was born and nurfed in the Hay-market, I was foon tranfplanted, and have thriven in reputation accordingly: The air of the Garden, and purlieus of Drury, agree with me as well, if not better, than my native air. And though, for divers reafons that I fhall not enumerate at prefent, I inhale the falubrious effluvia of Milk-alley—and have chofen the attick ftory for the purity of the atmof-phere to a naturally confumptive habit—Gra-titude to you, Gentlemen, compels me to defcend fome flight of ftairs to meet you on an equal footing, and throw the following little

Ruffle of Caution—Dalrymple Tactis, hem!—
moft humbly at your feet. You muft confider,
Gentlemen, you are defcending faft into the
vale of years; therefore much lenity fhould be
fhown towards men, who have hitherto, till
this prefent feafon, always acted with manly
confiftency, and never loft fight of their true
intereft till now—Partiality to children is ami-
able, when difcreet—Æfop himfelf played with
Boys, and Socrates diverted himfelf with the
youth of Athens—but *"tempora mutantur."*
Boys condefcend to play *with* you, and *upon* you,
and confequently with the Public at large.

Is he in fault? Or his parent? No—Who
then? Afk the enormous ftipend he has ex-
acted from your over-ftrained rivalfhip of out-
bidding each other! Whereas, had you con-
fulted Doctor Panglofs, a Doctor of Laws, an
eftablifhed Author, a profeffed Critic, a learned Philologift, and, to fum all in three letters,
an A.S.S. he would have advifed you to lay
your wife heads together, to offer a ftipulated
nightly fum of ten pounds, and one benefit at
each houfe, confiderably under the ufual charges,
in confideration of his tender years—and as encouragement—This would have been fully ad-

equate; and muſt have been accepted—For had you been firm, London being the objeſt to ſtamp him, he muſt have acceded to your terms—and if, as I hear it rumoured, that Drury-Lane managers have offered increaſed terms for next ſeaſon, I can only ſay, what Manly ſays to Sir Francis Wronghead; "If you have not quite made your fortune before, you have clench'd it now."

But what avails argument againſt prepoſſeſſion?—this is the age of wonders! the age of *infantine experience,* and *puerile maturity.* There

are *Comic* Rofcius's, infant *Billingtons*, and mufi-
cal Prodigies of eight years old—Mafter B——
will be *fuperannuated* in another year—Men and
women, formerly in the prime of life at thirty
or forty, are now Antediluvians; and from a
parity of Reafon, you muft confess yourfelves,
Gentlemen, from this evident partiality, to be
in your fecond Childhood.

     I am, Gentlemen,

        With true Efteem,

          Your old Friend & humble Servant,

            PETER PANGLOSS,

From my Attic Apartment,
     Milk-Alley.   L.L.D. & A.S.S.

YOUNG ROSCIAD.

A Certain Perfon now in town,

Whofe fon's a boy of much renown,

Born fomewhere, but it matters not—

Certain it is—he's not a Scot—

No *M——* he—nor *T——* neither,

But *gallops* falter on than either;

For while the former took fome *years*

Before their ev'ry act appears,

This cautious parent, as *chef d'œuvre,*

Accomplifhes by grand manœuvre;

And opes the public's eyes at laſt,

To wonder at a few *months* paſt.

 By "*Auri ſacra fames*" led,

Many a one has bravely ſped,

And for a time held up his head :

But Fortune is a fickle jade,

And Avarice is ſoon betray'd,

When public characters miſuſe,

And public confidence abuſe,

Whate'er their rank—whate'er their fame,

They're, *ipſo faƐto*, all fair game !

Oh, *Intereſt ! Intereſt !* partial god !

Who ſhow'rs down bleſſings at thy nod !

What wonders canſt thou not achieve,

*What make blind mortals not believe !

* 'Tis well known what uncommon interest was previously made for his reception, before Young Roscius' appearance in town; how he has been held up since, I

In politics and ſtate affairs,

John Bull is jealous of all ſnares ;

But when from *State* to *Stage* he turns,

All ſenſe and reaſon ſoon he ſpurns ;

Some faſcination by ſurpriſe,

Miſleads his ſenſes, ſeals his eyes.

What is the mighty magic, pray,

Has led poor *John* ſo much aſtray ?

'Tis *Faſhion*—Sir—howe'er abſurd,

There's mighty magic in that word !

Get but a *name*—no matter how—

Tranſcendant merit he'll allow.

shall no longer conceal from the Public.—" Born for your use—I live but to obey you—Know then—'twas *I* "——" But, Oh! what—what was my recompence !"

YOUNG's *Revenge.*

" I must confess—I feel myself somewhat *huff'd.*"   PANGLOSS.

Merit is *Fashion*—fashion *Merit!*

Synonimous with men of spirit.

Let but a great man take your hand,

With proffer'd service at command,

The multitude press close behind,

The adage prove—"Blind leads the blind !"

And so it is—from recent causes,

Else how would *Roscius* gain such 'plauses?

*The boy has certainly some points,

Expressive face and pliant joints,

But shou'd some years be kept at school,

Nor make the public such a tool.

---

* " For want of interest, I have been spinning out my brains these twenty-five years in Milk-alley.—I had once a prospect of a tutorship in a nobleman's family—Lord Duberley's, I think, but missed it, not for want of application and assiduity on my part—As I hear his father has lately dissmissed Mr. H—— with a most liberal annuity for life, I have serious thoughts of offering myself to amend the young gentleman's Orthoepy—which is very defective—Of this hereafter—*Verbum Sapienti*."

PANGLOSS.

All fober critics, fure, muft deem

It folly in a great extreme,

To vie with men, and to poffefs

More impudence than they profefs ;

No folly his—and hence it follows,

John Bull's the fool who tamely fwallows.

Can a boy feel thofe ardent fires,

Maturity alone infpires?

Can he *difcriminate*—conveying

New meaning to his parts in playing?

O yes ! undoubtedly ! his fenfe

Soars far above fuch vague pretence—

And what's the toil of many years,

In him all *natural* appears.

To him, by *Intuition's* given,

A fole exclufive gift from Heaven !

*Immaculate and Heaven-born boy !

†Thy father's prop—the public's toy !

The public are the generous factors

Of *Heaven-born Ministers* and actors,

Till time developes ev'ry scheme,

And JOHN BULL wakens from his dream,

Lo!—how he looks—he rubs his eyes,

And wildly flaring with surprise,

Searches his pockets—to his coft,

Finds all his ready rhino's loft !

---

* " I should not be surprised, if the roof of Drury-Lane Theatre were to fly off*—
and this *angelic* boy, were, like *Enoch*, to be translated into Heaven ! ! !"

                                        * * * * * * * *

†" C——— say so ? C———! a fool ! a fool ! fine boy ! fine boy ! no doubt———
but I prefer seeing men and women perform———"

---

* The roof fly off, &c.—" That would be a grand *Spectacle* indeed ! far superior
to *Cinderella*. It would certainly attract all the pretty *little-Misses* in town, and I
of course would be there." OLD Q. in the Corner.

By *Man* and *Boy* together drain'd,

Of what his induſtry had gain'd,

He ſtamps and ſwears, 'tis all deceit,

That old and young are both a cheat.

He wonders he is made the tool

Of *Scotsmen,* and a *Boy* from ſchool !

He vows, they'd better all be jogging,

For all alike deſerve a flogging.

*Ye *Kembles, Cookes,* pray keep aloof,

Nor enter under the ſame roof !

* " I certainly had a voice in engaging the *boy* for Covent-Garden, as I thought
the novelty might bring *grist* to the mill, wherein *I* have a ſhare—otherwiſe I ſhould
have ſtrongly oppoſed any ſuch innovation—he is certainly clever—but *Hamlet* he
ſhould not have attempted." K———E.

" I deny that, Mr. K———; his Hamlet is excellent—ſo is he in every other character but *Richard*—I am aſtoniſhed at his temerity in undertaking it." C———E.

" In my humble opinion, Gentlemen, he does ample juſtice to every part but
Young Norval. The author ſeems, however, to think otherwiſe—he ſays, ' he is the

Ye *Siddons*, *Johnstons*, *Popes*, give way,

And never more presume to play.

Ye twinkling stars, of lustre lack,

Retire at once, or stand far back.

" He comes ! he comes ! YOUNG ROSCIUS comes !

" Sound all, ye trumpets—beat, ye drums!"

This glorious Sun, in lustre bright,

Irradiates the dusky night—

E'en *Garrick's* ghost he keeps at bay,

It flits before him in dismay !

only Young Norval he ever saw.'—The venerable gentleman has forgot, no doubt,
that he passed the very same compliment to me some few years back ; but he is now
in his 86th or 87th year—that accounts for it."   J————N.

' " Psha Sheer—envy, by the Gods ! the very parts, Gentlemen, you object to,
are, in my mind, what he is most adapted for—but to attempt *Frederick* in Lover's
Vows, was the height of *folly*—call it by no worse a name—he has not *one* requi-
site for that arduous character."   P————E.

Never before the like has been,

Never before the like was feen.

This fprig, with confidence well lin'd,

Throws competition far behind.

With *men* you can't compare the lad—

That were unjuſt—they'd think you mad;

He has you there upon the hip;

Your fingers then upon your lip:

In filence be your thoughts immur'd—

What can't be help'd muſt be endur'd.

By Heaven! 'tis ſtrange this fafcination,

Or rather this *infatuation!*

That he, Coloffus-like, fhould ſtride,

Sweep all before him, like the tide.

But tides are wont to ebb and flow,

And once deceiv'd, we wifer grow.

c

Far be the wifh to check his fpirit,

And not allow him every merit;

That as a *Boy* he ftands apart,

And gains applaufe from ev'ry heart;

As fuch, encouragement is due,

Proportionate to him from you :

But when, without difcrimination,

Profufion's fcatter'd by the nation,

When rich and poor, and young and old,

All rufh to fill his bags with gold,

Unmindful of their former friends,

This—Juftice—Common Senfe offends.

Why accufe ftatefmen of undoing,

Plunging the land almoft in ruin,

When you yourfelves run headlong down

Each vicious vortex of the town?

When no expences ye regard,

Tho' all complain the times are hard?

Nor will ye in the fmalleft meafure,

Deny yourfelves one moment's pleafure.

No wonder then, fome greedy pike,

Snaps up the gudgeons when he like.

   Ye veteran Actors, who have reign'd,

And univerfal praife obtain'd,

Now what avail your toil and trouble ?

Your honours vanifh like a bubble !

What's *ten* or *twenty*, *thirty* years,

To pleafe the town ? it *nought* appears,

*When in *one* feafon this boy gleans

More than a *Life* behind the fcenes.

* It is calculated that, on the most moderate average, young Roscius will have realized, between the two houses, this season, including benefits, salary, presents, &c. &c. the paltry sum of ten thousand pounds !—" *Risum teneatis ?*"—They may laugh who win.   Pangloss.

" Is this juſt dealing, Nature, say—

" For him to carry boundless ſway ?

" Muſt we ſtand by—look tamely on,

" And ſee our *Bread* thus trod upon?

" Nor jealouſy—nor envy's fang,

" Tow'rds a mere boy, that gives the pang;

" More ſerious injuries we ſuffer,

" From this unprecedented puffer!

" *Our benefits may turn out *Minus*—

" Ay, *there's the rub!* then who will dine us ?

" Think of that, Maſter Brook, to grieve us,

" Dame Quickly'll truſt no more, believe us—

" Our friends, we fear, have turn'd their backs,

" Drain'd of their caſh by this *new Tax.*

* "My benefit has fallen far short of my expeɛlation, as it generally does from one cause or another—I must ask Master Betty the reason—and so must many more, I fancy." 　　　　　　　　　　　　　　　　　　　　　　R. W. E.

" From all such *impofition* fever us!

" And in due time, good Lord, deliver us !"

* Full many an *Author* joins the pray'r,

From deprivation of *his* fhare—

By little Betty's ftrange obtrufion,

They've fuffer'd for a time exclufion;

The *Public*, too, are difappointed,

And new productions left disjointed.

†Thus many a Bard remains in dudgeon,

Supplanted by this young Curmudgeon.

---

* " I am a melancholy witness of the fact: a comedy and a musical piece were to be brought out this season, but are shelf'd now till the next—Wherefore—ask Betty."
A. C.

† " My School for Reform, I am positive, would have run longer, had not Master Betty appeared so often—this is a serious loss in reputation, if not in pocket—I would advise him to return to *school*, and *reform* his manners there."
T. M.

" I shall certainly introduce this young curmudgeon in some impertinent character in my next comedy—that will most probably make the town swallow it."
R.

*Take courage, friends! the time draws near,

Things will *in ſtatu quo* appear.

No longer need you rail or ſcoff,

The *Novelty* is wearing off.

Young Roſcius is a new Religion,

And Johnny Bull—'tis *he's* the pigeon :

He'll ſicken ſoon at *Schiſm*—and then

†He'll ſoon come back to *Church* again.

Oh Johnny Bull! haſt loſt thy ſenſes,

To liſten to ſuch vain pretences ?

---

* " He shall not play at the Hay-Market this summer, I'm resolved—I hate mono-
poly—though he's a lad of genius—I confess I was much pleased with his performance
of that *Lusus Naturæ* of mine, *Octavian ;* it shows his judgment in selecting it, so ad-
mirably suited to his powers—Doctor Panglos insists his Kakology wants mending—I
dare not dispute the Doctor's authority—though I rather suspect he has an interested
motive in the assertion."   G. C. THE YOUNGER.

† Alluding to what *Quin* said of *Garrick ;* but with more truth and certainty, we
may venture the present prediction."   PANGLOSS.

The dupe of every fordid elf,

For while *you* bleed, they hoard the pelf.

Egad—they're right—'tis all fair play,

While the fun fhines to make the hay.

'Tis *you*, friend Johnny, are the fool,

Thus to be made th' egregious tool—

Well may you fhake your head and grieve,

They pocket *thoufands*—laugh in fleeve :

No thanks to boot from them to you,

To their *own Merit* all is due!

That you've a right, I'll not gain-fay,

To fpend your money as you may ;

But this is furely Rhime and Reafon,

For *Folly*—*this* is *not* the Seafon.

The times are hard, demand the wits,

Of every man to mind his hits ;

For while you inconfiderate heap,

And fuffer little Boys to reap,

Thofe favours better elfe beftow'd,

You lack at *home*, and *Strangers* load!

Your bounty fhould be more *piano*,

*'Tis greafing the fat fow *in ano!*

While little Mafter, fmiling, hoards,

And fcorns each brother of the boards.

This *Contumacy* wants reproof,

And Juftice fhould not ftand aloof:

Where is thy wondrous merit, Boy,

That thou exclufively enjoy

---

* " I cannot approve of the *delicacy* of the erudite author's expression—I would fain attribute it to an accidental *Lapsus Linguæ*—perhaps he intended, as he is particular in his Phraseology, to suit the action to the word, and the word to the action; but he should recollect, with this *special* observance, not to o'erstep the *modesty* of nature." CRITO.

Favours exceeding all due bounds ?

Of thy pretenſions, what the grounds ?

" *I am the Faſhion !*"—why, that's true—

That's all that can be ſaid of you.

*A *rara avis*—a black ſwan—

A little proud Phenomenon !

This adulation has quite ſpoil'd you !

By your attempting much, has foil'd you ;

For all the world can plainly ſee

That you and *Shakſpeare* can't agree ;

That is a ſtudy rather cramp,

Too much for genius of your ſtamp.

Your Sire ſhould liſten to advice,

But he's a man not *over* nice—

---

* " Here again I am reluctantly obliged to call the Doctor to order—he inadver-
tantly blends compliment with contempt—and so is guilty of a kind of solecism."

D   CRITO.

On money evidently doats,

So thrufts you down the people's throats;

So far—*you*'re not in fault, I fay,

For every dog fhould have his day.

You are the Idol for a while,

And can a liftlefs hour beguile—

The reigning theme, perhaps, at Brighton;

A fecond *admirable Crichton !*

In fhort, 'tis plain—when *you*'re at hand,

Perfection's felf is at a ftand !

Vain-glorious Boy ! too foon you'll know—

You'll foon difcern your friend from foe;

Your *real* friend you have difmifs'd,

*What follow'd?—why, you foon were *hifs'd.*

* " Doftor Pangloss, I am sorry to obscrve, descends from the dignity of a learned philologist to the scurrility of a disappointed tutor. He certainly has mixed an unusual

I muſt confeſs—I ſee it plain,

You want your leading-ſtrings again;

Your *Action's* good—in general, *juſt*—

Your declamation gives diſguſt.

To ſave you from a like diſaſter,

Engage ſome *Elocution* maſter;

For inſtance, *me*—I ſpeak the truth,

I'm noted for inſtructing youth;

My terms—three hundred pounds a-year,

And thoſe muſt *moderate* appear ;

Upon my ſoul, I can't take leſs,

I'm L.L.D. and A.S.S !

quantity of *Nut-gall* in his ink, and, I must say, deserves the *goose* himself for it."

.*CRITO.

* *Crito* is a sneering Cynic—' Let the *galled* horse wince, *our* withers are unwrung.'—Shakespear—I am not the person he alludes to ; I never was employed by Mr. B——, but don't despair of having that superlative honor.

PANGLOSS.

Before you *act*, learn how to *read*,

Some years of ftudy much you need ;

And for fome feafons play no more,

Next feafon, you'll be *quite a Bore.*

We pardon *now*—we'll *then* reject,

For much improvement we expect ;

This is the *general* voice—and *true*;

Obferve in time, or elfe you'll rue!

But much, I fear, I've gone aftray,

To give you counfel any way—

For felf-conceited—felf-poffeft;

Prefumption fills your little breaft;

*Ingratitude has mark'd you out;

And fuch a crime, all mankind fcout.

* Here I am forry, *truth* compels me to relate a *genuine* anecdote, which tends to,
confirm the above affertion. Some few weeks back, the Marquis of H———— was

What if a Noble condefcend,

As many have, to ftand your friend—

By fhowering guineas in your lap,

You feed on *Gold* inftead of *Pap* ;

If fuch fhou'd afk—" Where is the man,

And whofe inftruction raif'd the plan

with Master B—— in Mrs. J——'s dressing-room. The conversation turned on Mr. H——, his late preceptor ; the young Marquis asked young B—— ' If he did not miss his instructor?' ' Oh, not in the least, he was of little service to me.' ' Indeed!' returned the Marquis. ' Surely in acquainting you with the trick of the scene, the business of the stage, the entrances and exits, the O. P's and P. S's. he must have rendered you essential service, from his long experience in the profession.' ' Oh, that's nothing, no matter where and how I enter; when *I* am on, that's full sufficient ; I am sure to bring them down; I engross the whole attention of the audience.' So much for our *modest*, *grateful* young Roscius. I must here correct a mistake in the public prints ; it was not the sum of *Half* a Guinea, the father, Mr. B——, gave his Instructor over and above his stipulated allowance—No—let me do the gentleman all possible justice—it could not be less than a *One* Pound Note—to pay for an outside place, and supply him on the road to his future destination.——Old *Elwes* could not have given less.

The above anecdote I had from a person who was an ear-witness to the conversation, and on whose veracity I can place the most implicit reliance. PANGLOSS.

Of eminence, in your profeſſion ?"

What is your *modeſt, plain* confeſſion ?

Would I could drop the curtain quite

On your reply a recent night !

Shame on you, Boy—your words recal,

Or *Arrogance* will prove your fall ;

Confeſs your obligations—own

You ſtand in debt to H—— alone !

This ſelf-opinion may ariſe

From partial friends, misjudging eyes ;

But truſt me, 'twill impede your courſe,

And of much miſchief be the ſource—

Some little *Miſs*, perhaps, may riſe,

And equally the Age ſurpriſe !

Who knows, perhaps—ſome little Letty

May ſhare the ſpoil with Maſter Betty !

Nay—I can vouch, I know of *one*,

Whofe fure fuccefs I build upon;

Whofe *Lady Randolph*, *Juliet*, too,

May make you look a little *blue*.

The public's mind is apt to range,

Stocks vary conftantly on 'Change ;

And all the world will yield it o'er,

A *Female* claims protection more.

Many rebuff, no doubt, you'll find,

Unlefs you temper more your mind.

Learn *Modefty*—a charm in youth,

It fafcinates us next to truth ;

Nor flight my counfel—or *next* year,

*I'll treat you fomewhat more fevere ;

---

* " I don't know how that can well be ; the learned Doctor appears not only an
alarmift, but a *terrorift*—and towards the conclusion of *his* Poem—he *advifes*

For I've a wondrous rod in pickle,

Your pretty little Bum to tickle—

Nor let your judgment, as you grow,

Contemn what comes not from a foe.

Your *friend* I am—your *real friend;*

To Flattery I fcorn to bend.

Poor thoughtlefs boy ! you've much to learn,

'Tween Good and Evil to difcern ;

For Riches often bring a curfe,

Much danger in a heavy purfe ;

" *Contentus parvo*" is a boon,

You cannot practife it too foon.

compliments and *threatens* in a breath—strange heterogeneous mixture—but poor *Pangloss* was ever an *eccentric* character."   CRITO.

Retire awhile, and cultivate,

Retire—and live not thus in ſtate,

Retire—and cope not with the Great.

Then ſhall your modeſty be praiſ'd,

Your name with double luſtre raiſ'd—

A decent competence you've gain'd,

And all, as yet, by *grace* obtain'd.

Wait 'till ſome few revolving years,

Till ſettled manhood full appears ;

Then burſting like meridian ſun,

Complete the work you've well begun ;

Nor run your youthful ſtrength full ſpeed ;

Of eaſe—retirement—you have need !

Time to *improve*—for there is room—

Or what's to be thy future doom ?

Things more important claim your care

Than *but* to study as a *Play'r*—

Lay in a useful stock of knowledge;

For that you need not go to College;

While *I* am ready—close at hand,

*Your humble Servant at command.

Take this advice, my youthful Sir,

And do not hesitate—demur—

Nor treat my caution with your laughter;

For, trust me, you'll repent hereafter.

---

* " The Doctor, to his last, has an eye to his professional advancement; but I fear he has gone the wrong way, to work himself into the good graces of young Roscius's father; he must probably continue his speculations in Milk-Alley—though I must acknowledge the advice he gives is that of a true friend, and ought by no means to be slighted."   CRITO.

For 'tis my *privilege* to fcourge,

When good advice in vain I urge ;

The province of fatiric Poet,

To make you *feel*, and let you *know* it.

F I N I S.

Printed by J. Roach, }
Russel-Court. }

Just Published, in one Volume, Foolscap Octavo, embel-
lished with a beautiful Frontispiece, Price Five Shillings in
Boards—

THE SORROWS OF SEDUCTION,
A Poem in six Delineations.

'This little volume, which, as the Author says, passed from himself immediately
to his publishers, without any examination on the part of a friend, exhibits great
elegance of taste, and warmth of feeling. The first Poem, on Seduction, is well ma-
naged, and has many pathetic and beautiful passages.' *British Critic.*

'We have perused these Poems with pleasure, excited by the uniformly good sen-
timents which pervade them; by the love of religion, morals, and virtue, which is
displayed in almost every page. The Author has manifested taste in the Selection
of his imagery, and has shewn himself not destitute of genius.' *Anti-Jacobin Review.*

'This is a Poem of considerable merit, on an interesting theme, and is a praise-worthy
endeavour to engage the charms of Poetry in the aid of Morality; a service from which
they have been too frequently diverted. It consists of six *Delineations*, tracing the
fatal connexion of Maria and Lorenzo, from their first interview to the death of
the latter.' *Eclectic Review.*

———————————————

Just Published, the much-admired Ballad of—"With timid Air,
and cautious Foot, Young Spring."—With an accompaniment
for the Pedal-Harp and Piano Forte. The Poetry by the
Author of the above celebrated Poem. The Music by Mrs.
M. A. Bryan.

London: Printed for W. Gordon, 357, Oxford-Street; and to be
had at all the Music Shops in the United Kingdom.

Lightning Source UK Ltd.
Milton Keynes UK
UKOW07f1921190715

255407UK00004B/83/P